Take-Off!
What are ...?
SEAS AND OCEANS

Andy Owen and
Miranda Ashwell

Heinemann
LIBRARY

First published in Great Britain by Heinemann Library
Halley Court, Jordan Hill, Oxford OX2 8EJ
a division of Reed Educational and Professional Publishing Ltd.
Heinemann is a registered trademark of Reed Educational and Professional Publishing Ltd.

OXFORD MELBOURNE AUCKLAND
IBADAN JOHANNESBURG BLANTYRE GABORONE
PORTSMOUTH NH (USA) CHICAGO

Designed by Susan Clarke and Celia Floyd
Illustrations by Oxford Illustrators (maps pp.23, 25, 27)
Originated by Dot Gradations, UK
Printed in Hong Kong/China

04 03 02 01
10 9 8 7 6 5 4 3 2

ISBN 0 431 02348 4
This book is also available in hardack (ISBN 0 431 02343 3).

British Library Cataloguing in Publication Data

Owen, Andy
    What are seas and oceans?. – (Take off!)
    1.Ocean – Juvenile literature 2.Oceanography – Juvenile literature
    I.Title II.Ashwell, Miranda III.Seas and oceans
    551.4'6

Acknowledgements
The Publishers would like to thank the following for permission to reproduce photographs:
Aerofilms, p.17; Australian Picture Library/J. Carnemolla, p.4; Geoslides, p.8; Images Colour Library, p.6; Kos Picture Source, p.7; NRSC pp.22, 24, 26; Oxford Scientific Films/Ian West, p.19; Planet Earth, p.14 (Jiri Lochman); Rex Features/Huw Evans, p.18; Robert Harding Picture Library/Ian Griffiths, p.13; Royal Geographical Society p.15; Telegraph/F.P.G., p.9, p.10 (Norbert Wu), p.11 (Kurt Amsler); Tony Stone, pp.5, 12, p.20 (George Grogoriou), p.21 (Stephan Munday)

Cover photograph: Oxford Scientific Films/Scott Winer

Our thanks to Sue Graves and Stephanie Byars for their advice and expertise in the preparation of this book.

Every effort has been made to contact copyright holders of any material reproduced in this book. Any omissions will be rectified in subsequent printings if notice is given to the Publisher.

For more information about Heinemann Library books, or to order, please telephone +44(0)1865 888066, or send a fax to +44(0)1865 314091. You can visit our website at www.heinemann.co.uk

Contents

Some words are shown in bold, **like this**. You can find out what they mean by looking in the Glossary.

Seas and oceans

There are four oceans in the world – the Pacific, the Atlantic, the Arctic and the Indian Ocean.

Oceans are very large. The water is very deep. It will take this boat many weeks to reach land.

Pacific Ocean

The Pacific Ocean is the largest ocean in the world.

Seas are smaller parts of oceans. Seas are found near **coasts** and islands. Most of the world is covered by seas and oceans.

Oceans cover about 70% of the Earth's surface.

Islands

There is land even in the middle of the ocean.
Land with water all around it is called an island.

island   beach

An island in the Pacific Ocean.

The biggest island in the world is Greenland.

island

beach

An island in the Atlantic Ocean.

Islands can be large or small. Some islands have many towns and cities but others have no people at all. Some islands, like this one, have only a few people living there.

Cold and warm seas

Most of this iceberg is hidden under the water.

Water in the Arctic Ocean is so cold it turns to ice. These large blocks of ice are called **icebergs**. Icebergs float in the water.

Nearly 80% of an iceberg is under water.

The Great Barrier Reef grows in the sea off Australia. The coral is growing in the pale blue water.

coral

In some parts of the Pacific Ocean the water is shallow and warm. Coral grows here in large mounds called a reef. The **coral reef** is made of millions of tiny animals.

Deep and shallow

Most seas and oceans are very deep. The water gets darker and colder as the sea gets deeper. People can dive deep into the sea in a diving bell.

diving bell

A diving bell protects divers so they can breathe deep under the sea.

mask

flippers

Divers hold their breath to swim in shallow water.

Close to the land, the sea is often shallow and warm. Fish, coral and seaweed living near the surface get lots of light. People like to dive under the surface of the water to look at fish and coral.

11

Waves

Strong winds and huge waves make a storm at sea.

Strong winds whip the water into big waves. The waves get larger as they move across the sea. Boats and ships are tossed about by the storm.

breaker

breakwater

Waves called breakers crash onto the land.

The wind drives the waves towards the **coast**. The waves tumble and crash onto the land. We call the crashing wave a **breaker**. **Breakwaters** are built to try to stop the damage caused by breakers.

Cliffs

Waves hammer against the cliffs every day. Slowly, over many years, the waves **erode** the rock and make jagged shapes in the cliffs.

breaker

These cliffs have been eroded by the waves.

landslide

cliffs

Buildings fell down when part of
this cliff fell away in a landslide.

Over many years the waves weaken the rocks at
the bottom of the cliff. In the end the top of the
cliff falls onto the beach below. Sometimes land
above the cliffs slides and houses fall down.

Beaches

Waves roll sand, stones and pebbles around in the sea. Over many years, the stones and pebbles become smooth and round because of the waves.

Smooth stones and pebbles on the beach.

The waves carry sand along the beach. When the waves slow down the sand is dropped. Slowly a long strip of sand is made. This is called a **sand bar**.

sand bar

A sand bar at Spurn Head in England.

Pollution

Ships called tankers carry large amounts of oil. Sometimes oil leaks from the tankers and floats on the sea. We call this an **oil slick**.

oil tanker

oil slick

tug boat

This tanker was carrying oil from one country to another.

People cleaning oil from the beaches.

Oil pollution at sea is very hard to clean up. The waves carry the oil slick onto the beach. It harms **wildlife** on the **coast** and damages beaches.

Safe places

Harbour walls are built to keep out wind and waves. During a storm small boats are safe inside a **harbour**.

harbour

harbour wall

Harbours are safe places for boats on the **coast**.

Big ships can only use harbours with deep water. Places where ships load and unload are called **ports**. Sydney Harbour is a port and a harbour.

Sydney Harbour bridge

Sydney Harbour in Australia.

The Sydney Harbour bridge was built in 1932.
It is nearly 504m long.

Ocean map 1

harbour wall

harbour

This photo was taken from an aeroplane. You can see a small **harbour**. There are some boats inside the harbour.

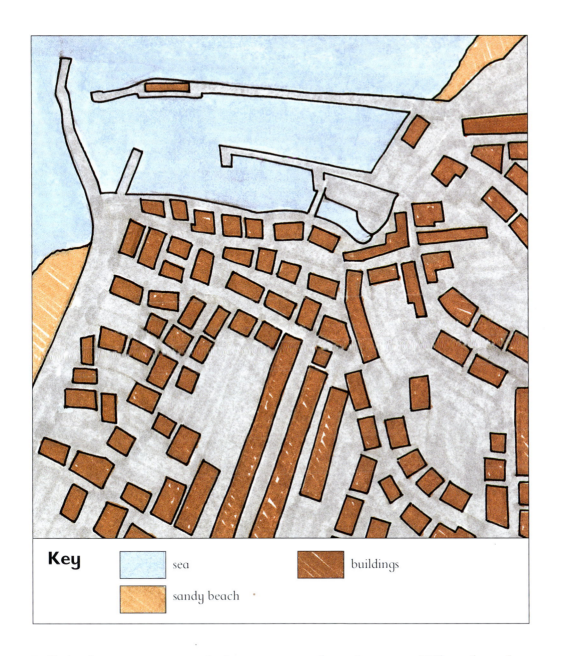

Key
sea		buildings
sandy beach		

This is a map of the same harbour. The harbour wall is shown. A map never shows boats because they move from place to place. Using the key, find the sea, the sandy beach and the buildings.

Ocean map 2

sandy
beach

shallow

water

This photo shows the same place. The **harbour** looks smaller, but we can see sandy beaches and shallow water on both sides of the harbour.

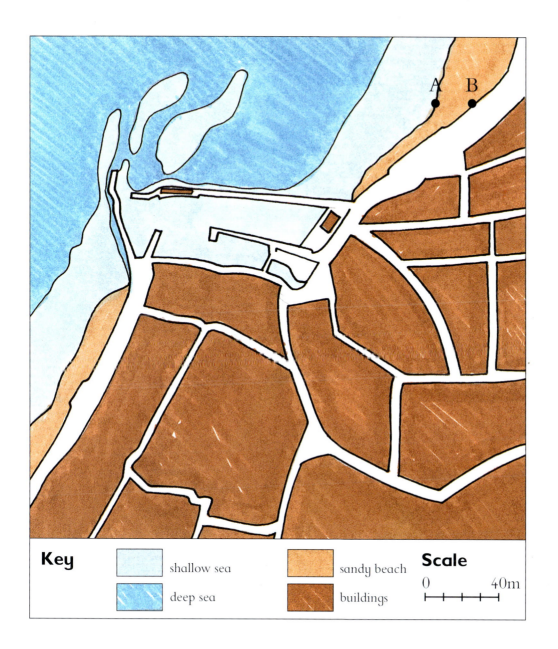

25

The key helps us to understand the map. It shows the things we can see on the photo. Light blue shows us the shallow water. Using the scale, find out how wide the beach is from points A and B.

Ocean map 3

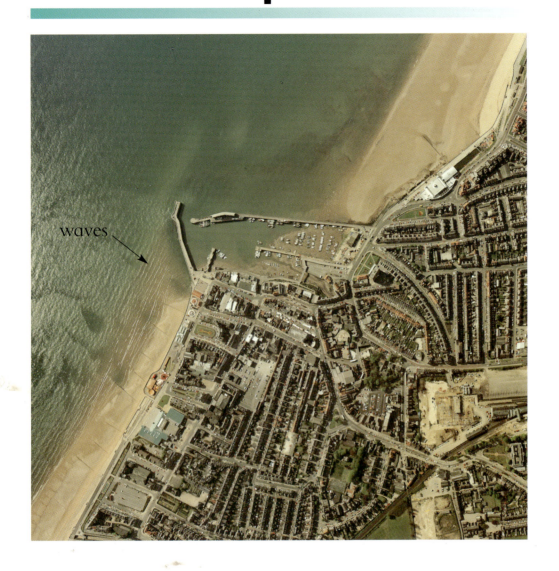

waves

In this photo we can see even more of the sea and the town. The sun is shining on the water which makes it easy to see the waves.

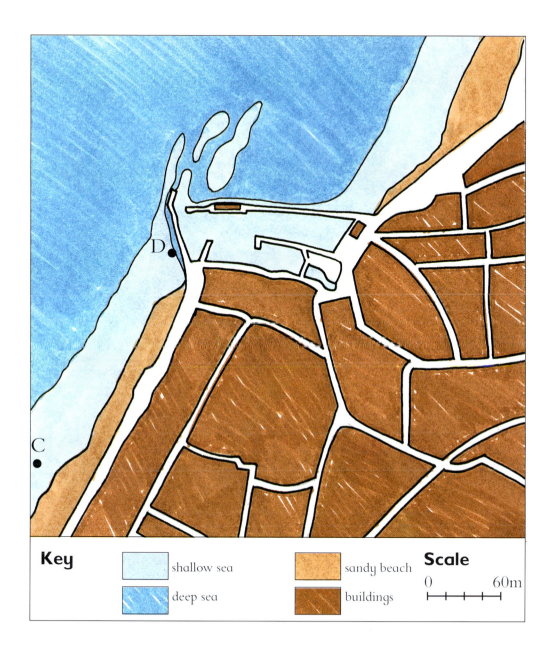

The waves are not shown on the map. This is because waves are always moving and changing. Using the scale, find out how wide the shallow sea is from points C to D.

Amazing ocean facts

The Great Barrier Reef in Australia is the longest **coral reef** in the world. It is 2000 kilometres long. The reef has taken 12 million years to grow.

coral

The largest ocean in the world is the Pacific Ocean. The deepest part of this ocean is the Mariana Trench which is 11 km below sea level.

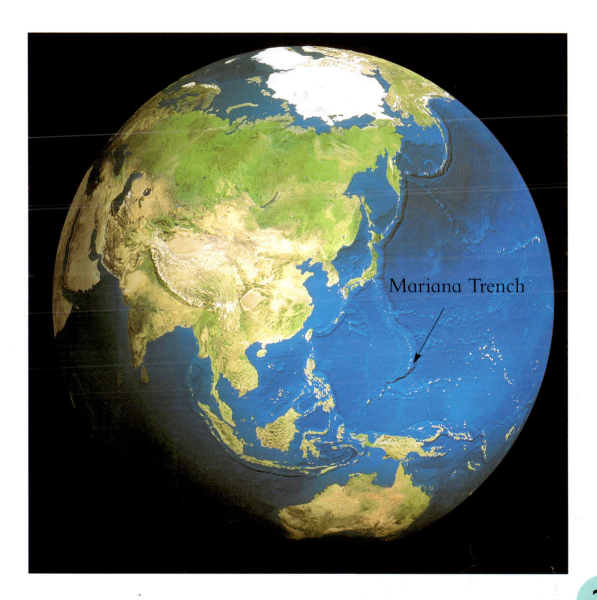

Mariana Trench

Glossary

breaker   a wave which crashes onto the land

breakwaters   structures, like walls, that break the force of waves crashing into the land

coast   the area of land near the sea

coral reef   tiny sea animals with a hard coat. They live in groups. Coral reefs look like strange shaped rocks

erode   wear away

harbour   a place on the coast where boats and ships are safe from rough seas

harbour walls   strong walls that protect the harbour from rough seas

icebergs   mountains of ice that float in cold sea

oil slick   large patch of oil floating on the water

ports   places where ships load and unload

sand bar   strip of sand in shallow water

wildlife   plants, animals, fish and birds

More books to read

Francesca Baines. *Ocean World*.
Two-Can, 1997

Patience Coster. *Step-by-Step: Seas and Coasts*.
Franklin Watts, 1997

Claire Llewellyn. *Why do we have?
Rivers and Seas*.
Heinemann Library, 1997

Joy Palmer. *First Starts: Oceans*.
Franklin Watts, 1996

Index